Introduction

Welcome to the world of history! In this book, we will explore the events and personalities that have shaped our world, uncovering the hidden stories and secrets of the past. From ancient civilizations to the rise of modern nations, you will be transported back in time to witness the events and personalities that have shaped our world. Through extensive research and analysis, the author reveals the truth behind the myths and legends of history. With its engaging writing and rich historical detail, this book offers a unique and enlightening perspective on the events and people of the past. So come along and join us on this exciting journey through the pages of history!

Table Of Contents

The Eighth Century

The Ninth Century

The Tenth Century

The First Century

The first century was a period of great change and upheaval. It was a time of transition from the ancient world to the modern world, as the Roman Empire expanded its influence and new ideas and religions emerged.

In the early part of the first century, the Roman Empire was at the height of its power. It controlled much of Europe, North Africa, and the Middle East, and its economy was strong. However, as the century progressed, the Empire began to decline due to internal conflicts and attacks from outside forces.

During this time, many new ideas and religions emerged and spread throughout the Empire. In the east, a new religion called Christianity began to take hold, challenging the traditional ways of thinking. In the west, a movement called the Enlightenment began, promoting the idea of individual rights and reason.

The first century was also a time of great artistic and cultural achievements. The Romans built impressive structures such as aqueducts and roads, and made advancements in science, medicine, and engineering. The arts also flourished, with writers, artists, and musicians creating works that continue to inspire and influence us today. Julius Caesar was a Roman statesman, general, and one of the most famous figures in ancient history. He was born in 100 BC and rose to become one of the most powerful figures in the Roman Republic.

Caesar was a skilled politician and military strategist, and he is best known for his military campaigns and conquests in Gaul (modern-day France), where he expanded the territories of the Roman Republic. He is also known for his reforms to the Roman calendar, which introduced the leap year and the concept of the month.

Caesar's political and military successes made him a popular figure among the Roman people, but they also made him enemies among the ruling elite. In 44 BC, he was assassinated by a group of senators who feared his growing power and popularity.

Despite his untimely death, Caesar left a lasting legacy. He is remembered as one of the greatest military leaders in history, and his reforms to the Roman calendar have had a lasting impact on the way we measure time.

Overall, the first century was a time of great change and innovation, laying the groundwork for the world we know today.

The major political forces of the first century were the Roman Empire, which was at the height of its power, and the various barbarian tribes and external forces that threatened its borders.

The Roman Empire was a vast and powerful state that controlled much of Europe, North Africa, and the Middle East. It was ruled by an autocratic emperor and was known for its military might, engineering feats, and complex legal and governmental systems.

Egypt was a powerful and influential state during the first century. It was part of the Roman Empire, and it was known for its rich culture and history, as well as its many contributions to science, medicine, and the arts.

The first century was a time of great change and upheaval in Egypt. The Roman Empire was at the height of its power, and it exerted a great deal of control over the region. However, the Empire was beginning to decline due to internal conflicts and attacks from outside forces.

Despite these challenges, Egypt remained a center of learning and cultural achievement. The city of Alexandria was a hub of intellectual and artistic activity, and it was home to many great thinkers and scholars. The city was also known for its impressive library and museum, which were considered to be the best in the world at the time.

Egypt was a vibrant and influential state during the first century, and it played a significant role in the cultural and intellectual life of the Roman Empire.

However, the Roman Empire faced many challenges in the first century. It was constantly threatened by barbarian tribes from the north and east, as well as external forces such as the Parthians and the Sassanid Empire. These threats, combined with internal conflicts and economic problems, contributed to the decline of the Empire in the later part of the century.

Overall, the first century was a time of great political upheaval, as the Roman Empire struggled to maintain its power and defend its borders against external threats.

The second century was also marked by the emergence of new philosophical and intellectual movements, such as Neo-Platonism and Stoicism, which challenged the traditional ways of thinking and paved the way for the Enlightenment in the following centuries.

The emperors of the second century were a diverse group of rulers who faced many challenges as they attempted to maintain the power and influence of the Roman Empire. The first emperor of the second century was Nerva, who ruled from 96-98 AD. He was known for his mild and conciliatory nature, and he sought to address the internal conflicts and economic problems that were undermining the Roman Empire.

The Second Century

The second emperor of the second century was Trajan, who ruled from 98-117 AD. He was a military leader who expanded the territories of the Roman Empire, and he is known for his many public works and building projects.

The third emperor of the second century was Hadrian, who ruled from 117-138 AD. He was a patron of the arts and a builder of cities, and he is known for his extensive travels throughout the Roman Empire.

The fourth and final emperor of the second century was Antonius Pius, who ruled from 138-161 AD. He was known for his mildness and his support of the arts and philosophy, and he is remembered for his successful administration of the Roman Empire.

Overall, the emperors of the second century were a diverse group of rulers who faced many challenges as they sought to maintain the power and influence of the Roman Empire.

During the second century, China was ruled by the Han Dynasty, which was a period of political stability and economic prosperity. The Han Dynasty was founded by Liu Bang, who became the first emperor of the Han Dynasty in 202 BC.

During the second century, the Han Dynasty continued to expand its territory and influence. It conquered many neighboring states and established a network of roads and canals to facilitate trade and communication. The Han Dynasty also developed a sophisticated system of governance, and it made significant advancements in science, technology, and the arts.

One of the major events of the second century in China was the rise of Confucianism, which became the dominant philosophical and ideological system of the Han Dynasty. Confucianism emphasized the importance of tradition, filial piety, and social harmony, and it had a profound impact on Chinese society and culture.

Overall, the second century was a time of great progress and achievement for China, as the Han Dynasty expanded its territory and influence and made significant advances in many areas.

The Third Century

The third century was a time of great change and upheaval in the Roman Empire, Egypt, and China. It was a period of political instability, economic decline, and religious and cultural change.

The major events of the third century included the Crisis of the Third Century (235-284 AD), the rise of the Sassanid Empire, and the emergence of new religious movements. In Egypt, Alexandria remained a center of learning and cultural achievement, and in China, the Han Dynasty continued to expand its territory and influence.

The Crisis of the Third Century was a period of political instability and economic decline that lasted from 235-284 AD. It was a time of great upheaval and change in the Roman Empire, and it was marked by a series of civil wars and external invasions that weakened the power and influence of the state.

The crisis began with the assassination of the emperor Alexander Severus in 235 AD, and it was followed by a period of political instability and civil war. Over the next 50 years, a series of short-lived and ineffective emperors ruled the Roman Empire, and the state was unable to maintain control over its territories.

Overall, the third century was a time of great change and upheaval in the Roman Empire, Egypt, and China. These events laid the groundwork for the world we know today.

The emperors of the third century were a diverse group of rulers who faced many challenges as they attempted to maintain the power and influence of the Roman Empire during a time of political instability and economic decline.

The first emperor of the third century was Septimius Severus, who ruled from 193-211 AD. He was a military leader who restored stability to the Roman Empire after the Crisis of the Third Century, but he is also remembered for his ruthless tactics and his persecution of Christians.

The second emperor of the third century was Caracalla, who ruled from 211-217 AD. He was known for his military campaigns and his building projects, but he is also remembered for his brutal rule and his persecution of Christians.

The third emperor of the third century was Alexander Severus, who ruled from 222-235 AD. He was a reformer who sought to address the problems of the Roman Empire, but he was ultimately unable to prevent its decline.

The fourth and final emperor of the third century was Aurelian, who ruled from 270-275 AD. He was a military leader who successfully defended the Roman Empire against external threats, but he was unable to prevent its decline.

Overall, the emperors of the third century were a diverse group of rulers who faced many challenges as they attempted to maintain the power and influence of the Roman Empire during a time of political instability and economic decline.

The third century was a time of significant scientific and technological progress. Some of the major scientific innovations of the third century included: The development of the astrolabe, an astronomical instrument that was used to measure the positions of the stars and planets. The creation of the first paper mill revolutionized the production of writing materials.

The development of the art of distillation, which allowed for the production of perfumes and medical remedies.

The creation of the first mechanical clock, which used a water-powered mechanism to measure time. The development of the concept of the universe as a whole, as described by the Greek philosopher and mathematician, Claudius Ptolemy.

[illegible]

ni nec tibi. sed diuidatur. Respondit rex: et ait

uiue infantem uiuum. et non occidatur. hęc est

mater eius. Audiuit itaq; omnis isr[illegible] iudicium qd

isset rex. et timuerunt regem. Videntes sapientiā

in eo. ad faciendum iudicium. Sec̄ s̄ euḡ scdm iohm.

tempr̄. Prope erat pascha iudęorum: et ascendit

solimam ihs. Et inuenit intemplo uendentes

et oues et columbas: et nummularios sedentes.

fecisset quasi flagellum de fun[illegible]lis: omnes eiecit

mplo. Oues quoq; et boues. et nummulariorū effudit

mensas subuertit. Et his qui columbas uendebant

Auferte [illegible] et nolite facere domum patris

The 4th Century

The fourth century C.E was a time of great change and upheaval in the Roman Empire. It was a period of political instability and economic decline, as the Empire faced internal conflicts and attacks from outside forces. One of the major events of the fourth century was the rise of the barbarian tribes, who threatened the borders of the Roman Empire. In 410 C.E the city of Rome was sacked by the Visigoths, a barbarian tribe from the north. The Visigoths were a Germanic people who had their own distinct culture and traditions. They were skilled warriors and skilled craftsmen, and they are known for their art and architecture. The Visigoths played a significant role in the history of the Roman Empire, and their culture continues to be studied and admired by historians and scholars today.

The first emperor of the fourth century was Constantine the Great, who ruled from 306-337 AD. He is best known for his conversion to Christianity and his issuance of the Edict of Milan, which granted religious tolerance to Christians and other minority groups.

After Constantine's death in 337 AD, there was a brief gap in the imperial succession, as the Roman Empire was divided among Constantine's three sons. The empire was briefly ruled by Constantius II, Constans, and Constantine II, but these rulers were unable to maintain control over the empire and they were soon replaced by other emperors.

The second emperor of the fourth century was Julian the Apostate, who ruled from 361-363 AD. He was a philosopher and a military leader who attempted to restore the old ways of the Roman Empire and to suppress the spread of Christianity.

The third emperor of the fourth century was Theodosius the Great, who ruled from 379-395 AD. He was a military leader who successfully defended the Roman Empire against barbarian invasions, but he is also remembered for his brutal persecution of heretics and his support for the Nicene Creed, which defined the official beliefs of the Christian Church.

THE FALL OF ROME- 5TH Century

The fall of the Western Roman Empire is traditionally dated to 4 September 476 CE. This was the day that the Germanic king Odoacer deposed the last emperor of the Western Roman Empire, Romulus Augustus. The fall of the Western Roman Empire marked the end of a period of political, economic, and military decline that had begun in the 3rd century CE. After the fall of the Western Roman Empire, Europe entered a period of political and cultural upheaval known as the Early Middle Ages. Odoacer established a new form of government in Italy and attempted to restore order and stability to the region. However, his rule was short-lived, and over the following centuries, a number of Germanic tribes invaded and settled in the former territories of the Western Roman Empire. These tribes, which included the Ostrogoths, Visigoths, Lombards, and Franks, established their own kingdoms and territories, and the political landscape of Europe became fragmented and chaotic. The Eastern Roman Empire (also known as the Byzantine Empire) survived for another thousand years, but the Western Roman Empire never regained its former power and influence. The Eastern Roman Empire (also known as the Byzantine Empire) survived for another thousand years, but the Western Roman Empire never regained its former power and influence.

The 5th century was a time of great change and upheaval in Europe. The Western Roman Empire, which had dominated the continent for centuries, was in decline, and its power was being challenged by a number of barbarian tribes.

In 410 CE, the Visigoths sacked the city of Rome, marking the first time in nearly 800 years that the city had been conquered by a foreign power. The fall of Rome was a devastating blow to the empire, and it marked the beginning of the end for the Western Roman Empire.

Meanwhile, in the East, the Byzantine Empire was growing in strength and influence. Under the rule of Emperor Justinian I, the Byzantines reconquered much of the territory that had been lost to the barbarian tribes, and the empire became a center of learning and culture.

The barbarian tribes, including the Visigoths, Ostrogoths, and Franks, also played a significant role in the events of the 5th century. These tribes, which had originally migrated to Europe from the east, carved out their own kingdoms and territories in the former lands of the Western Roman Empire. The political landscape of Europe became fragmented and chaotic, as these new kingdoms fought amongst themselves for power and territory.

The fall of Rome, the rise of Byzantium

A time of darkness, and uncertainty

The barbarian tribes, with swords and shields

Conquered the lands, and plundered the fields

The Vandals sacked the city of Rome

A once great empire, now a crumbling dome

The Goths and Franks, they carved their own

New nations born, from the ashes of the old

The world was changing, in the fifth century

A time of chaos, and instability

But out of darkness, came a glimmer of light

A new world dawning, a new age in sight.

The 5th century was a period of significant upheaval and change, with the collapse of the Western Roman Empire and the rise and fall of various kingdoms and empires in Asia. In Europe, the Western Roman Empire was plagued by internal instability and weak leadership, which allowed foreign invaders such as the Visigoths and Vandals to sack Rome and occupy important provinces. Attempts to regain control and defend against these invaders were largely unsuccessful, leading to the eventual collapse of the Western Roman Empire in 476.

In China, the period of the Sixteen Kingdoms continued, with the formation and collapse of small sub-kingdoms ruled by warring ethnic groups. Eventually, the Northern Wei dynasty was able to reunite the north of China, but the south was divided between the Liu Song dynasty and various other states. This marked the beginning of the Northern and Southern dynasties period in Chinese history.

In India, the Gupta Empire was invaded by the Huna peoples from Central Asia, and ultimately fell to their invasion. These Huna peoples may have been related to the Huns who devastated Rome during the same period.

6TH CENTURY

Chlothar I was a king of the Franks who ruled during the 6th century. He was the son of Clovis I, who had divided the Frankish kingdom among his four sons. When Chlothar inherited two large territories on the western coast of Francia, he embarked on a campaign to expand his realm at the expense of his brothers and neighboring kingdoms. He avoided open warfare with his brothers by cooperating with them to attack other lands, and sharing the spoils of these attacks.

Through his efforts, Chlothar was able to reunite Francia by surviving his brothers and seizing their territories after they died. However, upon his own death, the kingdom was once again divided among his four surviving sons. Chlothar had five wives, which was not uncommon among the Merovingian kings, who did not adhere to the Christian doctrine of monogamy. He was not particularly devout and even introduced taxes on ecclesiastical property.

The 6th century was a period of significant historical events and changes around the world. In Europe, the collapse of the Western Roman Empire late in the previous century left the continent fragmented into many small Germanic kingdoms that were competing fiercely for land and wealth. From this upheaval, the Franks rose to prominence and carved out a sizeable domain covering much of modern France and Germany. Meanwhile, the surviving Eastern Roman Empire began to expand under Emperor Justinian, who sought to restore Roman control over the lands that had once been part of the Western Roman Empire. He was able to recapture North Africa from the Vandals and made attempts to fully recover Italy as well.

In Asia, the Sassanid Empire reached its peak of power under the rule of Khosrau I. This marked the second golden age of the Sassanids, who had become one of the dominant powers in the region. In northern India, the classical Gupta Empire came to an end, largely due to invasions by the Huna peoples. In Japan, the Kofun period gave way to the Asuka period, which saw the introduction of Buddhism and the development of a centralized government. After being divided for over 150 years among the Southern and Northern Dynasties, China was reunited under the Sui dynasty toward the end of the 6th century. The Three Kingdoms of Korea also persisted throughout the century. In Central Asia, the Göktürks emerged as a major power after defeating the Rouran.

In the Americas, the Classic Period of the Maya civilization in Central America came to an end, and the city of Teotihuacan began to decline after reaching its peak between AD 150 and 450.

The birth of the last Islamic Prophet Muhammad is traditionally dated to the year 570. Muhammad was born in Mecca, a city in the Arabian Peninsula, and is considered by Muslims to be the final prophet sent by God to guide humanity. He received his first revelation from God at the age of 40, and over the next 22 years he preached the message of Islam, eventually establishing a community of believers in Medina. Muhammad's teachings, which are recorded in the Quran, form the basis of the Islamic faith, and his life and example are seen as a model for all Muslims to follow.

SACRVM IMPERIVM, EST FVN-
datum ſuper quatuor Ciuitates.

Ciuitas Auguſtenſis. Ciuitas Metenſis.

Ciuitas ſeu oppidū Imperiale Aquiſgrani. Ciuitas Lubicenſis.

Von den vier Stetten.

Vier Stet Sein dem heiligen Reich vor andern Stetten vor die fürnemyſten angenommen.
Die erſt Stat iſt Augſpürgk.
Die ander Metz.
Die dritt Ache.
Die vierde Lubeck.

7th Century: Empires a Falling

The 7th century was a period of significant historical events and changes around the world. In Arabia, the unification of the peninsula by Muhammad and the spread of Islam began, leading to the formation of the Rashidun Caliphate and the Umayyad Caliphate. Under their rule, Islam expanded beyond the Arabian Peninsula and conquered territories including Persia, Syria, Palestine, Armenia, Egypt, and North Africa. The

Muslim conquest of Persia in particular led to the downfall of the Sasanian Empire, which had been one of the dominant powers in the region.

In Europe, the Byzantine Empire suffered setbacks during the rapid expansion of the Caliphate but was able to retain its hold on Asia Minor after a decisive victory at the Siege of Constantinople. This victory was crucial for the survival of the empire, as it allowed them to retain control over a key strategic region. The Lombards maintained their hold on most of Italy, while North Umbria rose to dominance in the British Isles, establishing itself as the dominant power in the region. In the Iberian Peninsula, the 7th century was known as the "century of councils" due to the number of councils held in Toledo.

In Asia, the Sui dynasty was replaced by the Tang dynasty in China, which set up its military bases from Korea to Central Asia. This allowed the Tang to assert its dominance over a large region and expand its territory. China began to reach its height during this period, and Silla united the Korean Peninsula under its rule. In Japan, the Asuka period persisted throughout the 7th century, with the spread of Buddhism and the development of a centralized government. In India, Harsha united the northern regions, which had fallen into small republics and states after the fall of the Gupta Empire in the 6th century.

In the 7th century, great change did unfold,

With the rise of Islam, and the conquests that followed.

The Rashidun and Umayyad Caliphs did rule,

Expanding their empire, and making it whole.

In Europe, the Byzantine Empire did hold,

Despite setbacks from the Caliphate's grip bold.

The Lombards maintained their dominance in Italy's lands,

While Northumbria rose in the British Isles' strands.

In Asia, the Tang dynasty did take the throne,

Expanding its power, and making it known.

Silla united the Korean Peninsula, with might,

While in Japan, the Asuka period shone bright.

In India, Harsha did rise to power,

Uniting the north, and building a tower.

The 7th century was a time of great change,

With empires rising, and some rearranged.

A period of upheaval, and of shifting tides,

That shaped the course of history and forged its strides.

In India, Harsha united the northern regions. In Africa, the city of Timgad was destroyed by Berbers, and the religion of Shugendō evolved from a mixture of Buddhism, Taoism, and Shinto in the mountains of Japan.

The 7th century also saw the arrival of the Bulgars in the Balkans, leading to the establishment of the Bulgarian Empire. Arab traders also began to penetrate the area of Lake Chad. In Europe, the Sutton Hoo ship burial in East Anglia, England, was discovered, and the earliest attested English poetry was recorded.

In China, Buddhism was made the state religion, and unofficial anti-Christian persecution began. In Korea, the North-South States Period began. In Canada, the Mount Edziza volcanic complex erupted in northern British Columbia.

In Asia, the Sumatra-based Srivijaya naval kingdom flourished and declined and wet-field rice cultivation and small towns and kingdoms flourished. Trade links were established with China and India. In Indonesia, the Sojomerto inscription, written in Old Malay, was dated to around this time, and mentioned Dapunta Selendra, possibly the ancestor of the Sailendra dynasty. This suggests a link between the Srivijayan kingdom and this family.

In Africa, the Arabs captured Carthage from the Byzantine Empire.

The Eight Century:

The 8th century was a time of great change and upheaval around the world. In Europe, the Vikings began their raids on the coastlines of the continent and the Mediterranean, establishing powerful kingdoms in their wake. In Asia, the Pala Empire rose to prominence in Bengal, while the

Tang dynasty reached its height under the rule of Emperor Xuanzong in China. The Nara period began in Japan, marked by the construction of the first permanent capital city.

In Africa, the Umayyad Caliphate expanded its territory, conquering the Iberian Peninsula and North Africa. However, their expansion was halted at the Siege of Constantinople by the Byzantine Empire and the Battle of Tours by the Franks. The Classical Maya civilization in the Americas also began to decline during this time.

The 8th century saw the composition of the epic poem Beowulf, the formation of the first Serbian state, and the translation of Buddhist Jataka stories into Syriac and Arabic. The Giant Wild Goose Pagoda in Xi'an, China was also extended by 5 stories during this time, reaching its towering height.

In the 8th century, the world was a vastly different place than it is today. The Umayyad Caliphate, a vast Islamic empire, stretched from Spain to the borders of India. In the far East, the powerful Tang Dynasty ruled over

China, while in the Western world, the Frankish Empire was beginning to take shape under the rule of Charlemagne.

In Africa, the Ghana Empire was just beginning to rise to power, while in the Americas, the great city of Teotihuacan was in decline. It was a time of great change and upheaval, as powerful empires rose and fell, and new cultures and religions spread across the globe.

The early 8th century saw the rise of the Abbasid Caliphate, which would come to dominate the Islamic world for centuries to come. The Caliphate moved from Damascus to the newly founded city of Baghdad, which would become a center of trade and culture.

In Europe, Charlemagne was engaged in a long and bloody struggle with the Saxons, finally crushing their rebellion and incorporating Saxony into the Frankish Empire. In the East, the An Shi Rebellion devastated China, and Arab and Persian pirates burned and looted the city of Guangzhou.

The 8th century dawns bright and bold

With Arabs conquering far and wide

The Umayyad Caliph overthrown

And Baghdad rises as the new Caliphate's home

In western Africa, the Ghana Empire starts

While in the east, the Tang dynasty's art

Reaches its peak in the Great Wild Goose Pagoda's rebuild

And a camel carrying musicians, a sight so fine and skilled

Arab armies clash with Tang in the Battle of Talas

Central Asia falls, a great victory for the Arabs

In England, Offa rules with a steady hand

While in China, rebellion tears the land

Java launches raids on ports near and far

While Charlemagne battles the Saxons in the war

The 8th century a time of great strife

But also, a time of power and life.

The 8th century was a time of great change and upheaval. The Umayyad Caliphate was overthrown and replaced by the Abbasid Caliphate, which moved its capital to Baghdad and became a center of trade and culture. In Europe, the Vikings began raiding the coasts, leading to the founding of important kingdoms. In Asia, the Pala Empire was founded in Bengal and the Tang dynasty reached its peak in China.

In Africa, the Ghana Empire rose to prominence. In Japan, the Nara period began. Arab and Persian pirates and travelers burned and looted the Chinese city of Guangzhou, and the Tang Dynasty shut the port down for decades. The construction of the famous Indonesian Buddhist structure Borobudur began. Charlemagne invaded northwestern Germany and fought the Saxons for over thirty years, eventually crushing their rebellion and incorporating Saxony into the Frankish Empire.

The Second Council of Nicaea was set up to restore the use and veneration of icons, which had previously been suppressed. The Manjusri Rha temple was completed in Java, and the Kalasan temple was constructed. The Frisian-Frankish wars came to an end with the last uprising of the Frisians. Emperor Kanmu moved the capital of Japan to Kyoto, and Charlemagne was crowned the first Holy Roman Emperor by Pope Leo III. The Buddhist Sailendra kingdom flourished and declined. It was a time of great change and upheaval, but also of great progress and achievement.

In the year 778, the Kalasan temple was built

Its beauty and grandeur unmatched, its art and design a true delight

The intricate carvings and sculptures, a testament to the skill of its creators

And as the sun sets on its golden spires, it glows with an ethereal light

In the fields, the heavy plow is in use, tilling the fertile soil

As the farmers work tirelessly, their backs bent with toil

With the advent of the horse collar, the horses plow the fields with ease

Their progress swift and efficient, as they move with skill and finesse

In the east, the art of papermaking is introduced from China to the Arabs

A revolutionary development, that greatly improves the flow of ideas and words

And as the iron horseshoes come into common use, the horses gallop with renewed vigor

Their hooves pounding the earth, as they race towards their destiny with a roar

In the land of the Chalukya, the city of Pattadakal flourishes and thrives

Its architecture a fusion of styles, a true masterpiece of design

The Chinese monk Yi Xing applies a clockwork mechanism to his celestial globe

As he studies the stars and planets, seeking to unravel their mysteries and hidden truths

And in the land of the Picts, the first European triangular harp is designed

Its beautiful melodies filling the air, as it is plucked with skill and grace

The 8th century is a time of great progress and innovation

As the world moves forward, towards a bright and prosperous future.

:

The Ninth Century

The 9th century occurred during the years 800 –900 in accordance with the Julian calendar. It was a time of great change and upheaval in many parts of the world.

In Europe, the Carolingian Renaissance saw a revival of learning and culture, while the Viking raids continued to devastate the continent. In the Middle East, the House of Wisdom was founded in Baghdad, attracting scholars from all over the world. The field of algebra was founded by the Muslim polymath al-Khwarizmi.

In Southeast Asia, the height of the Mataram Kingdom happened in this century, while Burma saw the establishment of the major kingdom of Pagan. Tang China saw effective rule under Emperor Xianzong, but also faced the Huang Chao rebellions. The Maya civilization experienced widespread political collapse, leading to internecine warfare and the abandonment of cities.

Britain was greatly affected by the Viking expansion, with the Danes establishing themselves in the Heptarchy and creating the Danelaw. Ireland also experienced significant Viking raids, with the Vikings establishing longphorts along the coast. Scotland saw Viking incursions, leading to the collapse of the Pictish kingdoms and the rise of Kenneth MacAlpin as the first King of Alba.

In Africa, the Ghana Empire was founded in the west, while the Islamic world saw the rise of the Abbasid Caliphate and the end of the Umayyad Caliphate. The Chinese Buddhist monk Yi Xing applied a clockwork escapement mechanism to operate and rotate his astronomical celestial globe. The 9th century was a period from 801 (DCCCI) through 900 (CM) in accordance with the Julian calendar. During this time, the Carolingian Renaissance and the Viking raids took place. In the Middle East, the House of Wisdom was established in Abbasid Baghdad, attracting many scholars to the city. The field of algebra was founded by the Muslim polymath al-Khwarizmi. The famous Islamic Scholar Ahmad ibn Hanbal was tortured and imprisoned by Abbasid officials. In Southeast Asia, the height of the Mataram Kingdom occurred, while Burma saw the establishment of the major kingdom of Pagan. China began the century with the effective rule of Emperor Xianzong and ended the century with the Huang Chao rebellions. The Maya civilization experienced widespread political collapse and internecine warfare. In Britain, the Viking Age continued and the kingdoms of the Heptarchy were gradually conquered by the Danes. Ireland was also affected by Viking expansion, with extensive raids and permanent settlements being established. In Scotland, Viking incursions weakened the kingdoms of the Picts, leading to the eventual consolidation of power under Kenneth MacAlpin. The kingdom of Wessex, ruled by Alfred the Great, was the only kingdom of the Heptarchy to remain independent.

reland in the 9th century was organized into small kingdoms called tuatha, which were sometimes ruled by a single provincial ruler known as the High King if they were able to maintain authority over the tuatha.

Scotland also faced significant Viking incursions during the 9th century. The Vikings established themselves in coastal areas, usually in northern Scotland and the northern islands. The Viking invasion and settlement in Scotland contributed to the collapse of the Pictish kingdoms that inhabited most of Scotland at the time. Not only were the Pictish realms weakened or destroyed, the Viking invasion and settlements may have caused the movement of Kenneth MacAlpin, the king of Dál Riata at the time. After the death of Áed mac Boanta in 839, Viking incursions destroyed Dál Riata, leading MacAlpin to move east and conquer the remaining Pictish realms. MacAlpin became the king of the Picts in 843 and subsequent kings were titled as the King of Alba or King of Scots.

The 9th century was a period of great cultural and intellectual growth in many parts of the world. In Europe, the Carolingian Renaissance saw a renewed interest in classical learning and culture, leading to the establishment of institutions such as the Palace School and the creation of works such as the Einhard's Life of Charlemagne and the Nithard's Histories. In the Middle East, the House of Wisdom was founded in Abbasid Baghdad, attracting many scholars to the city and leading to the development of fields such as algebra by the Muslim polymath al-Khwarizmi.

In East Asia, the Tang Dynasty reached its height of power and cultural influence, with the construction of the Giant Wild Goose Pagoda in Xi'an and the development of the first printed book, the Diamond Sutra, using woodblock printing. In Japan, the Heian period began, marked by the development of the kana syllabaries and the rise of the imperial court and its culture. In Southeast Asia, the Pagan Kingdom flourished and declined, while in South Asia the Hindu Mataram Kingdom rose and fell.

H
in
of
m
of
of
ca
ar
H
fr
from the public expression

The Tenth Century:

The 10th century was a time of great change and upheaval across the world. In Europe, the period is often referred to as the "Dark Ages," as it was a time of war, famine, and social instability. In China, the Song dynasty was established, and in the Muslim world, there was a cultural zenith in places like al-Andalus and the Samanid Empire. Despite the challenges of the time, there were also cultural and intellectual flourishing in places like the Byzantine Empire and the First Bulgarian Empire. Overall, the 10th century was a complex and fascinating period in world history.

The 10th century was a period of significant cultural and political developments around the world. In Europe, the Byzantine Empire, which had its capital at Constantinople, experienced a cultural flowering, with notable achievements in art, architecture, and literature. The First Bulgarian Empire, which was located in the Balkans, also experienced a period of cultural and political growth during this time.

In the Muslim world, the Caliphate of Córdoba in present-day Spain reached its zenith, becoming a center of learning and cultural achievement. The city of Cordoba, in particular, was known for its libraries, schools, and hospitals, and was a hub of intellectual activity. The Samanid Empire, located in present-day Iran and Central Asia, also reached its peak during this period, with significant achievements in literature, science, and art.

In China, the Song dynasty was established in 960, marking the beginning of a period of political stability and economic growth. The Song period is considered a golden age of Chinese civilization, with significant advances in technology, art, and literature.

Despite these cultural achievements, the 10th century has often been referred to by historians as the "Dark Ages." This term was first used by Italian Renaissance scholar Caesar Baronius, who described it as the "Iron Century" due to its harshness and lack of moral goodness. Later historians have also used the term to refer to the relative lack of cultural and scientific progress during this period compared to earlier and later eras.

During the 10th century, Europe was still recovering from the collapse of the Western Roman Empire in the 5th century. Many of the continent's former Roman provinces had become independent kingdoms, and Europe was fragmented into a number of small states. This lack of political unity made it difficult for Europe to compete with the larger and more centralized empires of the Muslim world and China.

In addition to political fragmentation, Europe also faced a number of other challenges during the 10th century. Invasions by Scandinavian Vikings and Magyars, as well as conflicts between Christian and Muslim states, disrupted trade and caused widespread destruction. The spread of disease, particularly the bubonic plague, resulted in massive population loss.

www.ingramcontent.com/pod-product-compliance
Lightning Source LLC
LaVergne TN
LVHW052101160826
845678LV00015B/3310

9798368356358